Homeland Security Advisory Council

Countering Violent Extremism (CVE) Subcommittee

Interim Report and Recommendations
June 2016

CONTENTS

PREFACE

In November 2015, Jeh C. Johnson, Secretary of the U.S. Department of Homeland Security (the Department), directed the Homeland Security Advisory Council ("HSAC"), to establish a subcommittee ("Subcommittee") that is focused on Countering Violent Extremism ("CVE").[1] The Subcommittee was stood up to act as an incubator of ideas for the new Office for Community Partnerships (DHS/OCP), and has worked to leverage outside expertise and new thinking to support and enhance as well as assist in reframing and re-envisioning, where necessary the Department's CVE efforts.

Specifically, the Subcommittee was asked to address how the Department can best support non-governmental initiatives that either directly or indirectly counter violent extremism, including:

- Identifying opportunities or platforms useful for the Department's facilitation of public-private partnerships with both technology and philanthropic sectors
- The development of new networks and a framework for sustained dialogue and engagement with those partners to include non-governmental sectors
- Other non-governmental sectors, besides technology and philanthropic, that should be leveraged for CVE and how the Department should engage them
- How best to work with education and mental health professionals to help parents and schools understand how they can counter youth radicalization to violence
- How the Department can inspire peer-to-peer attempts to challenge violent extremism through public-private partnerships

This report focuses on the spread of violent extremist ideology and the recruitment of American youth to extremist groups, and how the Department can be a platform and an engine to leverage partnerships in the technology, health, education, communications, cultural, philanthropic, financial, and non-government sectors to counter such recruitment. While recognizing previous efforts – from those of the Spring 2010 Countering Violent Extremism Working Group to the more-recent Foreign Fighter Task Force – this report seeks to focus on discrete areas, separate and distinct than those undertaken in other efforts.

Subcommittee Findings

To effectively address and conquer the challenge of violent extremism, our nation requires the full engagement of our whole community, and entities across sectors. Chief among these elements are the American people and the American private, non-governmental and academic sectors, working in partnership with the government. Today, more than ever, we must harness the power of American ingenuity, creativity, and resilience. We must engage, activate, and align the private and non-governmental and academic sectors to address violent extremism, and the threat that it poses – in all its forms, across all communities.

---

[1] Please see Appendix #5 for CVE definition.

Subcommittee Members recommend a range of initiatives to support the Department's approach to the above focus areas, having solicited a broad array of views from leaders in the non-governmental, technology, philanthropic, public, health, and academic sectors.

Notably, the Subcommittee unanimously recommends significantly increasing staffing funding by as much as $100 million for both grants and program administration for the DHS/OCP – charged with implementing CVE efforts and representing the Department within the newly designated CVE Task Force. This funding would be used to develop a nationwide infrastructure of federal support to local community efforts, continue to spur innovation online and in the social sciences, and provide necessary grant funding to support non-profits and local governments in their CVE work. The current funding level of $10 million in FY16 for grant programs through DHS/OCP is insufficient to effectively counter the spread of violent extremist ideology in the United States, and does not in itself offer the chance to level – much less gain advantage against – increasingly aggressive efforts to recruit and radicalize our youth by violent extremist organizations at home and abroad.[2] Securing additional funding can help mitigate the threat of violent extremist ideologies but will require close and sustained coordination with Congress – potentially to include a new Congressional Liaison within DHS/OCP. This will include dedicated funding spanning all forms of violent extremism and funding for data and metrics such that future programing may be supported based on evidence.

Just as significantly, while many related national security challenges (such as public health or climate change)[3] receive funding for initiatives through private foundations and other non-profits, CVE receives very little. As such, in the immediate term, *all* of the weight of this challenge is on government to mobilize resources and encourage stronger private sector engagement. Given the credibility of non-government actors to achieve CVE objectives, and adaptive nature of private philanthropy, incentivizing their involvement will be paramount for success. Experts strongly recommend that government act quickly to enable a conducive environment for private sector action.

Many experts expressed concerns that funding is tied to the same agencies that have law enforcement mandates or that CVE stigmatizes some of the very communities it seeks to help, notably the American Muslim communities. As noted in the recommendations, addressing the core of these perceptions and otherwise creating incentives for private foundations to help address this challenge cooperatively is critical if we are to have a lasting impact.

This report seeks to catalyze efforts between the public and private sectors. The Subcommittee notes the need not just for a high volume of activities, but also for more targeted, professional, and comprehensive actions. Of note, better data analysis and use of

---

[2] Consistent with the understanding that $10 million is not sufficient, on May 26, 2016, the Senate Appropriations Committee reported out S. 3001, The Department of Homeland Security Appropriations Act, 2017 which provides $50 million for CVE grants for FY17. https://www.congress.gov/bill/114th-congress/senate-bill/3001

[3] The White House. Office of the Press Secretary. "Fact Sheet: The 2015 National Security Strategy." News release, February 6, 2015. The White House. https://www.whitehouse.gov/the-press-office/2015/02/06/fact-sheet-2015-national-security-strategy.

innovative measures of effectiveness will be important to ensure future efforts are evidence-based.

In addition, a common theme that underlies the majority of recommendations is the need to recognize the cultural and technological trends shaping identities of Millennials and to directly engage them in efforts.

Also notable is what the government should *not* do, such as to act as the messenger (as opposed to *empowering* "credible messengers" or "influencers"). Further, government must avoid stigmatizing specific communities or those seeking mental health services and ensure adherence to the privacy restrictions inherent in The Privacy Act and The Health Insurance Portability and Accountability Act (HIPAA).

The use of social media and technology are part of the challenge, the Department must fully understand and leverage social media in its policy and programmatic activities. To generate new ideas and bring additional expertise to the Department's CVE work in this sector, the Subcommittee spoke with a range of experts in digital marketing and branding, technology, and social media.

The United States Government must take all forms of violent extremism and radicalization seriously, prioritizing those forms that pose the greatest threats to safety and security, most urgently.

Ultimately, the approaches this report recommends for the Department will help it evolve over time and adapt to the changing nature of violent extremism itself, namely, the convergence and alliances of violent extremist groups across the full spectrum of grievances: To include those that espouse and/or undertake violence justified through various ideologies, to include anarchists, sovereign citizens, white-supremacists, and others.

The subcommittee believes that the U.S. Government needs to build mechanisms for animating state, local, civil society, and the private sector as key enablers to adapt to this new era of challenges. This report seeks to assist in that effort. Based on these themes, and in light of the functional areas requested by the Secretary for examination, the Subcommittee respectfully submits the following recommendations.

EXECUTIVE SUMMARY

The Countering Violent Extremism (CVE)[4] Subcommittee of the Homeland Security Advisory Council (HSAC) engaged with a wide range of experts and leaders to assess the status of efforts to counter violent extremism in the Homeland. Based on their input, the Subcommittee is making recommendations to expand on non-governmental partnership principles referenced in the HSAC Foreign Fighter Task Force Interim Report, Spring 2015. Specifically, the Subcommittee recommends:

➤ **Strengthening the Department to Do the Job:** The Department is significantly under-resourced to provide the activities and programming to stem online and offline radicalization and recruitment to extremist violence in the United States. A clear-eyed view of the threat before us, which the Subcommittee recognizes, requires an immediate *and* significant increase in funding and other resources – including possibly new authorities – for the Department to accomplish its goals.

Key Recommendations
- Strengthen the Office for Community Partnerships by immediately increasing funding and authority
- Redesign infrastructure of communications to take into account new technologies and methods being used by the non-governmental sector
- Given the evolving threat and how the process of radicalization itself is evolving, update and change the rules on how government uses lexicon
- Invest in deeper and more deliberate data analysis and more well-trained professionals in government to coordinate efforts efficiently
- Develop partnerships with the Departments of State, Education, and Health and Human Services to build new lines of interaction on CVE programs
- Strengthen partnerships with State, Local, Tribal and Territorial law enforcement stakeholders to ensure connectivity and coordination on CVE efforts.

➤ **Focusing on a National Architecture Across All 50 States:** Given that we live in an open and democratic system, and regardless of ideological persuasion, the threat of violent extremism does not recognize U.S. jurisdictional boundaries – state and local, national or tribal. The Department must be aggressive about building the necessary networks nationally. Existing efforts that have proven effective must be scaled up. Our approach must be focused on the power of government to encourage and unleash our greatest strengths. The private, non-governmental sector – including the full range of civil society across *all* communities, working hand-in-hand with leaders in science, faith, and technology – and with the full endorsement of our elected leaders at all levels offers the best chance to counter the threat of violent extremism for future generations.

---

[4] In this report, CVE is defined as actions to counter efforts by extremists to radicalize, recruit or mobilize followers to violence and to address the conditions that allow violent extremist recruitment and radicalization

Key Recommendations

- Scale existing partnerships with the non-governmental sector that are already funded by government and have proven to be effective
- Establish new strategic partnerships with the private sector
- Catalyze new networks with the philanthropic and financial sectors
- Create and leverage networks and professional associations of mental health and social services organizations to create scalable partnerships with the philanthropic sector
- Partner and expand national networks of mayors and governors.

➢ **Prioritizing Attention on the Millennial Generation:** Our nation's youth are at risk of online radicalization and recruitment like never before. They are by far the largest demographic being targeted by extremists, especially online. It is therefore our duty to protect them. Prioritized attention to the generation under 30 years old (digital natives across race, religion, ethnicity, location, socioeconomic levels, ideology, and gender) is required to prevent violent ideologies from influencing this segment of our population.

Key Recommendations

- Prioritize attention on efforts to counter the recruitment of youth to violent ideologies across race, religion, ethnicity, location, socioeconomic levels, and gender
- Establish partnerships for collaboration with the Department of Health and Human Services and Department of Education to address a range of pathways to recruitment, exchange of best practices and lessons learned.
- Scale up platforms (social media, technology, new, and emerging media) to encourage private sector creation of more and more targeted online content and micro-targeted distribution channels
- Partner with public and private colleges and universities across the country

In this report, the Subcommittee lays out a conceptual framework for the Department and offers specific actions that should be taken to leverage its strength, address areas of improvement, and provide a way forward that is measurable and comprehensive. This report offers the Secretary of Homeland Security a clear assessment of what must done in the short and long term. The recommendations herein are paramount to keep the Department appropriately adaptive to the new generation of threats to the Homeland related to the threat of violent extremism.

I.   THE DEPARTMENT: SETTING US UP TO DO THE JOB

Background

Based on consultations with a wide range of experts, the Subcommittee recommends that the Department of Homeland Security develop a comprehensive organizational plan to address the issue of the rising appeal and impact of violent extremist ideologies to domestic audiences. This will require significantly scaling the Department's footprint and capacities to engage civil society and the private sector. Our investment must match our rhetoric and rise to the generational challenge that we face, so that words can translate into concrete and measurable action. In order to do so, the Department must look inward to change the way it speaks to itself and the world and to invest in best practices that catalyze research and harness the full spectrum of American technology and creativity to take on this challenge while, at the same time, looking beyond government to identify partners-as well as resources- who can assist in this effort.

The Subcommittee urges the Department to recognize its strategic strengths as an institution in fulfilling its objective, including acting as convener and facilitator, and as a thought leader and intellectual partner to prioritize what is working. Building the right platforms and networks across U.S. society and facilitating connectivity with non-governmental partners presents an appropriate role for the Department as it seeks to engage a new generation of change-makers. In order to empower such momentum, the Department must have clear leadership and direction, with a broad footprint to complement non-governmental actors. With inspiration from a wide variety of experienced organizations and people ranging from non-profits, entrepreneurs, business leaders, and those within government, progress towards defeating violent extremist ideologies is possible.

Recommendation 1: Strengthen the Office for Community Partnerships

Context:

In September 2015, Secretary Johnson established DHS/OCP to "build relationships and promote trust, and, in addition, find innovative ways to support communities that seek to discourage violent extremism and undercut terrorist narratives."[5] DHS/OCP is charged with leading the Department's CVE efforts and with serving as the inaugural chair of the interagency CVE Task Force.

Given its central role within both the Department and the interagency, DHS/OCP is well suited to lead the efforts described throughout this document, and will require significant new resources to do so. Despite increased public and policy focus on CVE, federal funding has not matched the scope of this very real and present challenge. The initial national CVE strategy released in 2011, "Empowering Local Partners to Prevent

---

[5] Department of Homeland Security. Statement by Secretary Jeh C. Johnson on DHS's New Office for Community Partnerships. September 28, 2015.

Violent Extremism in the United States"[6] provided unfunded or under-funded roles and responsibilities for federal, state, local, and community partners on prevention. For five years, the Department has been placed in the untenable position of implementing a national strategy with no new funding. In FY16, for the first time, Congress allocated $10 million dollars to the Department for CVE grants, and $3.1M for the establishment of the office; it should move quickly to hire staff for DHS/OCP and efficiently and effectively dispense grant funding, including establishing new mechanisms for moving federal funding immediately to effective partners and programs.

In January 2016, Secretary Johnson announced the creation of the permanent interagency CVE Task Force which is responsible for bringing together personnel from across the executive branch to ensure that the challenge of violent extremism is faced in a unified and coordinated way. The CVE Task Force's work is important and integral to the success of CVE efforts. To this end, since all of the domestic focused recommendations, particularly those that are operational in nature would be best carried out by DHS/OCP.

Actions:

1. Establish DHS/OCP as the Secretary's CVE office, ensuring its leadership reports directly to the Secretary.
2. Significantly increase funding to DHS/OCP and authorize it to distribute funds to state, local, and non-governmental actors.
   a. Provide DHS/OCP with $100 million per fiscal year in funding. This funding will be used for CVE grants for programs and networks implemented across the nation. This would include office infrastructure, field staff expansion, and program resources.
3. Formalize DHS/OCP's role as the single CVE coordinator for the Department and a single point of contact to facilitate ease of dialogue between non-governmental entities and the Department.
4. Extend the mandate of the HSAC CVE Subcommittee to serve as a standing partner to DHS/OCP, the Department's Private Sector Office, and the Department in implementing the recommendations of this report and facilitating input and engagement from outside subject matter experts.
5. Establish regional offices around the country to facilitate DHS/OCP partnerships across state and local jurisdictions.
6. Formalize a partnership for a DHS/OCP Innovation Lab modeled after the State Department and Defense Department's similar efforts.[7] The Lab should facilitate the full range of efforts related to innovation and partnerships with technology innovators.
7. Task DHS/OCP and the Department's Private Sector Office to:
   a. Aggressively implement a philanthropic development strategic plan to provide ways for regional philanthropic fundraising for

---

[6] The White House. "Empowering Local Partners to Prevent Violent Extremism in the United States." August 2011.

[7] Pellerin, Cheryl. DoD's Silicon Valley Innovation Experiment Begins." *U.S. Department of Defense*. 29 October 2015. *and Department of State, Bureau of Political-Military Affairs, Strategy Lab*

community programs, working with the new Philanthropic Advisor to the HSAC (see Section II, Recommendation 2).

b. Build new access points for American companies, social entrepreneurial organizations, and educational institutions to contribute to CVE in-kind and otherwise.

c. Build on what we have done overseas and remodel it for the American context. Seizing the best ideas and content on all aspects of CVE from other agencies and departments –and other countries – requires new lines of interaction with the State Department, USAID, and Voice of America (See further: Section III, Recommendation 2).

Recommendation 2: Redesign Infrastructure of Communications

Context:

The changing nature of technology and the access it provides to ideas, notably the type and volume of violent extremist content and efforts to recruit youth to violent extremism has created an evolving challenge and opportunity. We are struggling to keep up with its pace and impact. Importantly, the process of radicalization begins at an individual level and relies on a constant feed of reinforcing ideologies that are spread both on and offline. Looking at the way ideas are spread in both domains is vital to our efforts. Local communities are central to understanding not only the origin but also the impact of changes taking place within neighborhoods, among peer groups, and as a result of influencers. In the online space, extremist groups have mastered the facility of integrated systems of communication, globally and at a scale and pace that has surpassed our current efforts to dominate the playing field. Their 24/7 efforts require us to be equally as constant and we must engage on this challenge on a level that is commensurate. With numerous forums wholly dedicated to messaging hate, current counter-narrative efforts are insufficient to keep up in time or volume of content. We must address the challenge of micro-targeting by our adversaries, which puts an onus on communities and the private sector to help confront and counter in creative ways.

In the case of foreign fighters seeking to join groups like ISIL, the Subcommittee sees the potential of a significant chapter ahead. A March 2015 Brookings Institution report suggested that ISIL supporters used approximately 46,000 Twitter accounts worldwide.[8] According to the Department's Center of Excellence, the University of Maryland's National Consortium for the Study of Terrorism and Responses to Terrorism (START), in 2002, the Internet was a factor contributing to the radicalization of 37% of the foreign fighters and aspirants who attempted travel to conflict zones to fight on behalf of terrorist organizations there. By 2015, the Internet contributed to the radicalization of 86% of those attempting travel since 2005, and 83% of the same in 2015 alone. Half of the individuals used the Internet and other technology tools as their primary source of information about traveling to the conflict zones. Further, approximately half of the

---

[8] Berger, J.M. and Morgan, Jonathan. "The ISIS Twitter Consensus: Defining and describing the population of ISIS on Twitter." Brookings Institution. The Brookings Project on U.S. Relations with the Islamic World. March 2015.

successful travelers maintained an active presence on social media, most often using social media to encourage others to travel, document experiences, and share tips for evading law enforcement detection. The data indicates that 20% of individuals attempting travel had established relationships with online travel facilitators who helped arrange safe houses and escorts to conflict zones.

American youth are not immune to this and there are increasing efforts to recruit young Americans to violent extremist ideologies. The nature of social media and the way extremists seed their ideas means that our communication system must be specific to the American context. The Department must adapt to this new era while amplifying our knowledge of how extremists lure youth offline in more traditional means. Arguably our nation has extraordinary possibilities of saturating the on and offline space.

Actions:

1. Leverage private sector expertise and best practices for deploying technology, communications, and marketing across mediums:
   a. Bring private sector talent into the government through the Department's Loaned Executive Program to assess and provide recommendations on communications and marketing efforts to support the CVE mission, including how to design measures of effectiveness.
   b. Institute a new exchange program whereby the Department's professionals can embed with technology, marketing, and communications companies for short periods of time to learn expertise and build relationships; this can be accomplished through the Exemplar Program authorized through the Department's Private Sector Office.
   c. Appoint "Technology Advisers" who are employed in the private sector but who are able to work with and provide expertise to the Department through the HSAC CVE Subcommittee.
   d. Build mechanisms for the exchange of best practices and lessons learned from the media and technology sectors on the creation of adjacent and native content for persuasion.
2. For the Department to help support the efforts of non-profit programs and organizations working to address messaging, technology, and communications issues by identifying one dedicated point of contact within DHS/OCP to convene non-profit and the private sector stakeholders to further the Department's and OCP's work in this field.
3. Appoint a new Member to the HSAC who works for a communications, branding or marketing agency and has a range of relevant experience in media and related industries.

Recommendation 3: Change Our Lexicon by Shifting How We Speak with Each Other and the World

Context:

The term CVE was developed to describe soft power tools focused on countering and defeating the ideology of violent extremists. It encompasses the range of communications, community engagement, mental health, and related practices that may reduce ideological, psychological, or community-driven factors conducive to support for violent extremist ideologies. In recent years, the term has moved into new spaces and has created unintended implications. CVE is not hard power, and it is not an investigative tool for law enforcement. Regardless, there is now a great deal of confusion among a new generation of government officials and civic leaders about what it means, what actual CVE programs do, and how to measure their impact. Recognition of this problem is critical, but it is possible to begin to change the perception and reclaim the original intent.

There are several layers to the issue around lexicon in the context of CVE. On the one hand, it might seem obvious to change the term CVE because there is a perception about its meaning that securitizes relationships between government and – in particular – Muslim communities. This results in credible influencers rejecting work that at all connects them to CVE. On the other hand, reformulating a new term that is agreed upon by the inter-agency and community groups could take years and is unlikely to yield a sustainable consensus. Subcommittee members do not recommend that the Department engage in a process to redefine CVE itself. Instead, the Subcommittee recommends focusing on immediate steps now that can help engage the full range of actors in the private and non-governmental sectors across communities in our nation.

There is a disagreement among scholars, government officials, and activists about the right lexicon to use around the issues of violent extremism. At the same time, report after report has recommended that the U.S. Government be consistent in its language and its meaning, highlighting that tone and word choice matter. Under no circumstance should we be using language that will alienate or be disrespectful of fellow Americans. Thus, we need to be clearer in what we mean and how we say it. Further, we are at a particular moment on the world stage with global events driving fear, political and cultural rhetoric leaning on sharp and divisive language, and deep polarization and distrust across communities. All of this is set against the backdrop of digitally connected recruitment efforts that are actively trying to exploit differences and create divisions across U.S. society. We must speak with honor and respect about all communities within the United States. We should give dignity to the many histories and diversities within our nation and advocate for a consistent whole of government approach that utilizes agreed terms and words. Tone and word choice matter.

Mental health experts and educators connect the environment we live in to emotional and physical well-being, behavior and issues of identity, belonging, and security. Words are part of that environment. Often without knowing it, we have constructed language in daily use that promotes an "us and them" narrative of division. Though it was within the context of the "War on Terror," the Department's 2008 guidance about lexicon is important to review as it has bearing on groups like ISIL. It instructs the Department to ensure terminology is "properly calibrated to diminish the recruitment efforts of extremists who argue that the West is at war with Islam."

In condemning violent extremism in all forms, we must also be better at communicating with the public and within government. In sum, we are in a complicated and challenging chapter: more people know we need to fight the spread of extremist ideologies but many do not know what we mean when we say we want to do that through CVE programs.

Actions:

1. Renew efforts to describe CVE, its origin of soft power,[9] and attempt to re-establish the term to ensure that prevention programs are not inter-mingled with surveillance or intelligence-gathering programs.
2. Bring consistency into government use of language and meaning.
3. Ensure the Department reviews the 2008 directive and uses a vocabulary when discussing extremism that avoids the "us versus them" framing.
4. Reject religiously-charged terminology and problematic positioning by using plain meaning American English.
   a. US v THEM: For example, use "American Muslim" rather than "Muslim American"; "Muslim communities" rather than "Muslim world."
   b. AMERICAN ENGLISH: For example, on using American English instead of religious, legal and cultural terms like "*jihad,*" "*sharia,*" "*takfir*" or "*umma.*"

Recommendation 4: Investing in Deeper Research and Data Analytics

Context:

In the 15 years since 9/11, there has been a significant amount of research in the field of extremism including how extremist groups prey upon young people, what techniques they use, and which types of messages resonate. We must be ahead of the curve and understand these trends. This means we need research and data that will give us the information we need to build a long-term CVE infrastructure that is evolved and adaptive.

We have seen new aspects to the threat emerge, like women radicalizing, and, compared to what we know about foreign populations and radicalization, there is limited data on American youth and their vulnerabilities. Moreover, as important as research focused on the entire scope of the radicalization process is, we do not have complete information around the measurement and evaluation of programs that intend to stop the

---

[9]Soft power can be defined as the ability to persuade rather than coerce to achieve a desired end. See Nye, Joseph S. "Soft Power." *Foreign Policy*, no. 80 (1990): 153-71.

appeal of extremists' ideologies. As such, we need to construct more effective tools to allow greater access to CVE research, and comprehensive and open source data. The Department must act as a catalyst to promote more aggressive research and analysis and find ways to collaborate with non-governmental experts doing such work.

Actions:

1. Catalog all CVE programs within America (see map in Appendix 3) – both government-funded and independent – to create a comprehensive and transparent overview of what exists in America and where gaps might exist. Remarkably none exists anywhere.
2. Assess the scope of work that exists on youth between 7 and 30 years of age regarding education and the process of violent extremist radicalization.
3. Develop clear measurements of impact based on the nature of the threat before us, and utilizing private sector approaches to measurement.
4. Build a practicum of research on the connectivity between other forms of extremism such as hate speech, cults, and other related issues.
5. Ensure there is a research focus on offline efforts to radicalize, including offline efforts that support online recruitment.
6. Catalog communications efforts and strategies currently underway that seek to provide counter, alternative, or proactive narratives by key stakeholders so that there is greater connectivity in the collective research. Stovepipes must be broken down.
7. Reduce redundancy in research and analysis. Facilitate cohesive purpose between the Department and the Department of State and other government entities to have access to and utilize U.S. Government-funded research and knowledge about U.S. Government funded programs abroad, and better understand approaches, lessons-learned and successes from our international partners.
8. Pioneer research around content from diverse communities within America, using this information to design and develop counter-narratives and bespoke programs for specific communities.
9. Redirect more research around gender differences, including child and adolescent behavior.

II. BUILDING AN ARCHITECTURE FOR ALL 50 STATES

Background

No region in the world is immune to the ideology of violent extremists and America has not been immune from terrorist attacks inspired by violent extremist ideologies. Rapid technological evolution and aggressive peddling of extremist ideology of all kinds suggests that extremist groups are exposing America's children to an unprecedented array of techniques, narratives, and tactics to radicalize. Although the United States has powerful advantages to fortify ourselves against the spread of violent extremist ideology, including our traditions of community activism and awareness on and offline, there has been significant growth in the ability of violent extremists to scale their efforts. In addition to a rise in hate-related crimes and speech reported across the country, there are open investigations by law enforcement agencies on American citizens in all 50 states targeting groups like ISIL.

We must scale up our efforts proportionally to ensure that future generations have the capacity and tools to stem the appeal of violent extremist ideology and thus, diminish the threat of terrorism in our own nation. We do not have the luxury of time. We must help create a new system of awareness, resilience, and understanding around extremism and the violence that comes from it. We must include all aspects of the trajectory to radicalization and develop a comprehensive response to the threat we face. To date, we have not built a nationwide architecture that integrates all that we know about radicalization and its prevention. As a result, efforts are ad hoc, disparate, under-funded, and sometimes redundant or counter-productive.

Efforts to counter extremist violence overseas since 9/11 has cost the United States over $1.6 trillion.[10] Funding in FY16 represents the first time ever in the Executive Branch that the Department will fund $10M to support and expand locally led efforts to implement CVE programing. There is no guarantee from the Congress that these funds will continue to grow in the FY17 budget request. Such funding is woefully low and has left us with a domestic approach that is segmented and insufficient.

The Subcommittee believes that the U.S. Government needs a national CVE plan that looks at the spread of ideology and its impact, which is distinct from a particular terrorist threat and its intersection with law enforcement. Because we know that cross-border communication and transit are easier than they have ever been, all states and localities must be part of addressing the challenge of violent extremism. In order to do so, the U.S. Government – notably DHS/OCP – must have the platforms to coordinate and communicate with partners locally, and those partners must be viewed as central components of an integrated system of networks. These networks run across all segments of society, from faith leaders to cultural icons, from mental health and science experts to teen entrepreneurs to philanthropists and corporations, to parent-teacher networks.

---

[10] Belasco, Amy. "The Cost of Iraq, Afghanistan, and Other Global War on Terror Operations Since 9/11." Congressional Research Service. December 8, 2014

The U.S. Government's ability to be the convener and facilitator, catalyze new networks, and pioneer new relationships with the non-governmental sector is essential to the success of creating a new American roadmap to build resilient communities.

Empowering local mayors and governors by giving them the insights, ideas, and information they need, along with linkages to best in class experts and organizations will be a game changer. The Subcommittee urges a nationwide approach to CVE, tailoring particular components in line with the individual cities and towns.

Recommendation 1: Build and Expand Platforms, Networks and Partnerships:

Context:

In order to expand to a nationwide footprint, we must create partnerships, platforms, and networks across states and localities. Notably we must invigorate non-governmental partners who have the expertise, skills, and credibility to construct a comprehensive approach to national CVE awareness and understanding around radicalization and recruitment. Further, as non-governmental people and systems are often the best practitioners of CVE programs, widening the connectivity across expertise areas will allow for innovation, creativity, sharing of best practices and coordinating efforts. New national platforms, networks and partnerships will allow us to quickly scale up our efforts and impact key areas.

Individuals in the marketing and technology industries have informed the Subcommittee of their interest in contributing time and expertise to this challenge. Many of CVE's challenges would benefit from this expertise, particularly counter-messaging and empowering communities; but, given restrictions on government accepting gifts or in-kind donations, a new approach must be imagined so that these partners can contribute.

Digital marketing experts have a sophisticated set of tools and methodologies that are proven to work, such as discovering a range of relevant information, creating, branding and marketing compelling content, and tracking real-world metrics to identify the most effective content for further distribution. Therefore, outside entities can be far more effective in leveraging digital marketing best practices than the government and if connected to non-governmental organizations can make a difference to achieving CVE objectives.

Family members, close friends, teachers, and clergy are often the first to notice that their loved one or friend is showing a warning sign of radicalization. According to a Federal Bureau of Investigation (FBI) report, in more than fifty percent of terrorist cases, family members see signs of radicalization but few consider a call for help. Finding ways to bring both experts and the general public into the CVE community is paramount for success. In short, we must create mechanisms to allow this critical group of people to both get help for their loved ones and find ways to seek counsel.

State and local government, especially in the prison system, and those who have experience and understanding around these issues have seldom been brought into the larger conversation and lack mechanisms to make that happen. There is an important continuum of law enforcement, the judiciary, and the corrections systems that must be incorporated into CVE efforts. Working in partnership with key departments and agencies, DHS has the capacity to help create a common understanding of the challenges of CVE and the potential opportunities for cooperation.

Finally, educators, schools and networks of parents and teachers, as well as organizations that impact youth, have had little to no connectivity to issues around radicalization and should be brought into the fold.

Actions:

1. Create mechanisms for the exchange of ideas and expertise on CVE beyond just the Department and include, potentially, the Departments of Education and Health and Human Services so that their extensive networks can add to our understanding of how violent ideologies are permeating across communities.
2. Create partnerships with cities and states to develop training and toolkits on CVE best practices. Leverage current networks of mayors and governors to develop working partnerships and strategies, and share best practices.
    a. Utilize existing networks such as the U.S. Conference of Mayors and National Governors Association.
    b. Work with the State Department to strengthen the Strong Cities Network for a national network of mayors and Governors in the United States.
3. Partner with public and private colleges and universities across the country. Scale up access to information on CVE by building a comprehensive CVE curriculum and create partnerships with universities nationwide so that "innovation labs" around CVE may be stood up.
4. Facilitate a network of corrections officials and re-entry service providers to identify the prison radicalization risk and spearhead rehabilitation best practices.
5. Develop demonstration programs that partner service-providers, faith-based actors, and local government to other localities. Take best practices from around the world to understand how such partnerships may be created and scaled up.
6. Create an information-sharing network for mental health, faith-based organizations, community centers, social work, and law enforcement actors, ensuring partners with access to sensitive information use separate servers with respect to HIPAA compliance.

Recommendation 2: Mental Health and Social Services Partnerships

Context:

Remarkably, though we know that understanding the child and adolescent mind is critical to understanding the radicalization and recruitment process, the U.S. Government has not built a formal system of accessing the very best data, research, and experts on a regular basis. Because developmental experts consider adolescent and young adult brain development and cognition to continue until roughly age 26, adolescence stretches into adulthood.[11] As recruits to violent extremist groups get younger and younger, and ISIL in particular is curating precise content for youth at specific stages of development, we are woefully behind in bringing the very best our nation has to offer into protecting our youth. Even further, we have not built any substantive outlets for youth to access help as they find themselves being drawn into the ideology, nor have we sufficiently offered America's parents a way to get help for their children as they perceive a change in their behavior. Consulting with mental health experts seems obvious, but there is no regular system in place to do so nor have we connected the world-class medical expertise in this field to our understanding about radicalization and extremism. We need to "complicate"[12] the thinking of adolescents around decision making, appeal to their individuality, openly discuss radicalization rather than avoid it, and understand their thinking on and impact of emotional impulses. It is rare to find partnerships between those that work on CVE and these medical and scientific experts who can help build more targeted and effective programs.

The subcommittee believes that the U.S. Government must do far more with our mental health sector. We have reached out to almost every other sector in America and we must execute a new chapter and partnership with the health sector, broadly speaking. Child and adolescent mental health resources must be a part of the architecture to protect our nation's youth so as emerging adults develop their worldview and subsequent behavior they have the tools needed to be resilient to the appeal of violent extremist ideologies.[13] [14]

Actions:

1. Work with leading hospitals and medical schools nationally to convene a high level group of researchers from psychology/psychiatry whose work specifically addresses violent extremism and those whose work could inform important aspects of CVE.
2. Create a system of ongoing dialogue between mental health sector experts with those in the policy sphere, and support dialogue between those doing research in the field and those designing content and distribution channels to reach our youth.
3. Create a new dynamic and innovative center by using an existing mental health venue (hospital, child-mind institute, research center, etc.) to bring together every element and dimension of the challenge. America needs a place that is the leading

---

[11] Interview with subject matter experts from Massachusetts General Hospital

[12] Term was presented and explained to the Subcommittee during conversation with subject matter experts from Massachusetts General Hospital.

[13] Additionally, researchers at World Health Organization (WHO) recently concluded that 27% of the adult population has experienced at least one mental disorder in the past year – the best way to tackle this concerning trend is through prevention early in childhood development. Thus, a national approach that focuses on children and young adults on and offline will provide the best opportunity to help prevent our youth from finding extremist ideology appealing.

[14] Clinicians have also noted that we should not adopt "the simplistic notion that mental illness could act as a marker for potential assassins, when psychotic illnesses are relatively common and assassins are extraordinarily rare." That is, we should not regard those who are seeking mental help as a "pool" of potential lone actor terrorists, not only because it is inaccurate, but because it could stigmatize those being in therapy and deter people who need help from seeking it, which could have serious consequences for the individual and his or her environment.

touchstone on how to help teens and young adults by understanding what is happening in the mind and that connects the behavioral, medical and scientific expertise on this issue.

      a. Part of this center will use BioPsychoSocial[15] and Socio-Ecological[16] frameworks in addition to several critical domains, including social bonds, identity, marginalization, discrimination, trauma, civic engagement/youth voice, individual and community resilience, and community engagement as well as participatory research including in-group and out-group dynamics and online behavior research.

      b. In each of these spheres, it is also important to think not only about risk/protective factors but how people have translated this knowledge into interventions that work. The center can be a place that can offer a holistic analysis of what is happening to teens and young adults and ways communities can get help as needed.

4. Create a network of grassroots organizations that counsel and disengage, using health, family, and social work resources, modeled on successful programs in other countries, but tailored to the U.S. context.

5. Create a national hotline for rapid intervention teams in the event of a radicalization concern.

6. Utilize the vast array of programs that already exist for other purposes, such as reducing juvenile crime, countering gangs, and preventing violence. We must develop a keen understanding of the mental health progression from childhood through adulthood with this particular kind of threat, incorporating CVE goals into existing mental health programs rather than having to consider creating new programs from scratch.

Recommendation 3: Catalyze Efforts in the Philanthropic and Private Sectors

Context:

Non-governmental actors can play a significant role in generating ideas and expertise, networks, momentum, and substantive funds to tackle problems that once were perceived to be the sole responsibility of government. Cause related philanthropy has built momentum among Millennials and interestingly, cultural icons from finance, tech, music and film have championed causes to fight child exploitation, including the plights of child soldiers and child slavery. Despite this fact, the issue of radicalization and recruitment of young people has not yet been a mainstream topic of philanthropy.

---

[15] BioPsychoSocial - Psychology/psychiatry often takes a "biopsychosocial approach to understanding health and illness. And more specifically considers how psychological (i.e., emotions, feelings, thoughts, behaviors), social (i.e., socioeconomic status, culture, societal context) and biological (i.e., genetics, basic neuroscience processes, physiology) factors and their complex interactions influence health and behavior.

[16] The Socio-Ecological model considers the complex interplay between an individual and his/her levels of social ecology (e.g., family, friends, school, neighborhood, nation, culture). This model highlights the range of social contexts/factors that a person lives within and that may make him/her vulnerable or serve to protect him/her. This model emphasizes that each level of one's social ecology influences another and therefore can be an opportunity for invention and will ultimately have impact across levels.

Ironically, it is this very sector that is needed most in order to scale up local ideas to fight the recruitment of youth for several reasons. Through seeding new ideas and creative approaches, increasing the power of ongoing projects or building new momentum, these kinds of private resources are very powerful. To inject alternative spaces and ideas into communities that are vulnerable, it takes organic and local initiatives to resonate because they are trusted.

Unfortunately, despite the seriousness of the threat of extremists, and the increase in fear and awareness in America that extremist ideology is increasing, non-governmental sectors continue to give little funding to organizations or initiatives that deal with this threat. Indeed, we have not seen the non-governmental sector realize its potential in providing funds to protect youth from violent extremists.

Despite the attempts at very high levels, there have been few major foundation initiatives or notable individual philanthropists who have initiated a new wave of philanthropic giving to communities who want to protect youth from the appeal of violent ideologies. The common perception that "government has money" or "it is a government problem" from potential donors has resulted in serious challenges and slowed the scaling up of effective local CVE programs. Local grassroots efforts, which could have the most impact, have difficulty accessing the needed resources to execute their ideas at scale. Organic ideas in the social media sector that beg to be tested require money. Professionalizing the fight against extremists in the ideological space requires more resources and, at present, the American effort at the grassroots is insufficient compared to the significant and growing threat posed by extremists preying on youth. However, while we have seen lots of money flow to other cause related philanthropy, American donors and civic investors have not yet taken on the issue of the spread and impact of extremist ideology.

At the same time, the evolving challenge of micro-targeting by our adversaries puts an onus on communities and the private sector to help confront and counter in creative ways – and these communities require resources to be activated and grow.
Government has a role to play in catalyzing private resources and leveraging limited government money to encourage more private resources to focus on this challenge. We also must find mechanisms that can move resources and funding quickly to private sector partners who are working at a pace commensurate with our adversaries to counter the threat in real time. Speed of funding is important and this may require a reexamination of vetting processes to streamline and create momentum where possible.

The new era of this threat requires a proliferation of local programs across the nation in a wide variety of ways to protect our nation's children, and Americans must be made aware for the need for non-governmental money to achieve this common goal. America has over 120 million youth under age 30. There are less than five small regional U.S. Government funded programs that deal specifically with stopping the appeal of groups like ISIL, a handful of experimental initiatives in the pipeline, and limited private donation to this cause. Things must change.

Actions:

DHS/OCP and the Department's Private Sector Office to carry out and coordinate:

1. Place personnel within philanthropic organizations, modeled after the USDA supply chain coordinator program.[17]
2. Build regional philanthropic plans of action and activate a corps of volunteer, expert fundraisers to help community stakeholders access funds by partnering with experienced philanthropic advisory organizations.
3. Appoint a philanthropic advisor as a new Member of the HSAC and task the HSAC to develop a follow-on report on private philanthropy supporting CVE.
4. Facilitate networks between philanthropic organizations and non-governmental organizations that are seeking funding.
   a. Seek legal guidance on what role is appropriate for the Department in these types of meetings.
   b. Examine vetting processes and funding mechanisms to ensure they are the quickest possible so that momentum and speed are encouraged.
   c. All meetings should be open to the public to ensure transparency in the process.
   d. Encourage non-profits to share best practices for fundraising, development, and building credibility.
5. Convene actors and encourage the creation of philanthropic hubs for funding content creation and distribution channels for online programs. Engage and utilize selected foundations focused on the threat of violent extremism as third-party vehicles for the Department to engage in funding and support of online and offline grassroots efforts directly. Foundations acting as intermediaries for government funding to these organizations can help activate a broad spectrum of technology innovators, local organizations and expertise.
6. Examine federal gift regulations to ensure the government may welcome private sector contributions that may reduce extremism.
7. Incentivize a generation of social entrepreneurs focused on these issues, through tax incentives, seed funding, and rewarding change-maker successes.
8. Explore creating a consortium of technology companies which can partner with the Department on content development, share best practices in the industry, and provide expertise on how best to develop counter extremist messaging, including preventing technology platforms from being used for violence and violent extremist recruitment.

---

[17] Interview with Eric Kessler, Founder, Principal and Senior Managing Director, Arabella Advisors. May 11, 2016.

III.   GENERATIONAL THREAT

Background

The Millennial Generation in the United States (those born between 1982 and 2000) now represent a quarter of the nation's population, exceeding that of the Baby Boomer generation.[18] Millennials are also the most diverse generation compared to any of those that preceded them – 44.2 percent of Millennials are part of a minority race or ethnic group. Notably, the population currently under 5 years of age is a majority-minority generation, illustrating the diversity the next generation of adults represents. The Millennial generation are digital natives, yet they are influenced both on and offline. Their exposure to news, world events, and each other, profoundly affect their ideas, behavior, and worldviews. Naturally, connectivity to their peers globally is an important characteristic of this under 30 generation. Beyond simply recognizing that they are unique in the way they use social media to interact and influence each other, this digitally connected generation is the prime target for extremists. The American Freedom Party (AFP), a white supremacist group, recently established a youth wing,[19] and they are not alone in doing so. Further, youth-focused wings of extremist organizations allow young people to draw in their peers and to facilitate youth-friendly marketing strategies. It is working. In the last few years, we have watched as youth in our country and globally are being radicalized at a concerning rate, crossing lines of race, nationality, socio economic status, ideology, education, and gender.

Researchers confirm that the median age for those recruited and radicalized to become foreign fighters for ISIL is 26 years old,[20] with the Internet playing a primary or contributing role in almost all radicalization processes. Even further, because extremists have developed kid and young adult friendly content, we must focus our attention on the online space. However, because youth are influenced by peers and move along emotionally through one-to-one persuasion, we also need to create an offline approach that is community driven and generational friendly. Effecting change in the environment means that we have to build a 24/7 comprehensive approach to influencing this generation. In order to do so, we must mobilize a range of efforts to protect them from recruitment and radicalization. Together with national networks of experts, peer influencers and credible content producers we can have enormous impact now. Stopping recruitment means expanding our understanding of the threat to this generation from diverse groups. We must restructure our national CVE efforts toward a framework that is attune with this demographic and design a system of influence on and offline that can significantly diminish the appeal of extremist ideology.

Recommendation 1: Protection/Predator Awareness

---

[18] 2015 Census Bureau Report.

[19] "Racist Group Begins Youth Recruitment Effort." *Anti-Defamation League*, January 12, 2015. http://blog.adl.org/extremism/white-supremacist-group-begins-youth-recruitment-effort.

[20] Program on Extremism at the George Washington University. Report. "April 2016." Accessed May 25, 2016. https://cchs.gwu.edu/sites/cchs.gwu.edu/files/downloads/April Report Update.pdf.

Context:

The Department's CVE efforts are an attempt to protect our nation's young people from extremists who prey upon the Millennial generation.[21] The Department must reframe the conversation to reflect this reality and design a robust program around the protection of our youth, which must include predator awareness and an understanding of radicalization. In doing so, our citizens will be better equipped for this threat. Because family members, close friends, teachers, and clergy are often the first to notice that their loved one or friend may become radicalized, public awareness is a critical first step.

Significant collaborations forged with tech companies and other non-governmental and local community partners over the years have resulted in a willingness to facilitate Internet safety and related educational and awareness efforts. With parents as the first line of defense, we must work with our partners to teach parents how to identify extremist ideological recruitment and also to teach them what to do in the event that they believe their child is radicalizing. Using all aspects of influence, we must find community spearheaded approaches to be responsive to America's parents and children.

Actions:

1. Develop a curriculum in partnership with the Department of Education and education experts and non-profits to disseminate to schools, teaching children appropriate online etiquette to mitigate online hate.
2. Create an action plan with the Department of Education to provide the training and expertise to school superintendents and others about radicalization.
3. Create a network connecting technology solutions to non-profit organizations and small businesses whose missions or interests overlap with CVE but lack the technical expertise, branding, and marketing, to actualize their full impact potential.
4. Build a network of parents who can collaborate on related issues, such as grassroots organizing to raise awareness of and raise funds for efforts to prevent online predators.
5. Build a network of mothers by partnering with existing organizations to scale up efforts for innovation and awareness.
6. Develop a Peer Mediation and Training Program through the National Crime Prevention Council (NCPC) for peer mediation and training related to violent extremism in all of its forms.

Recommendation 2: Providing Alternative Outlets and Counter Narrative Content

---

[21] Johnson, Secretary Jeh. "Remarks by Secretary of Homeland Security Jeh Johnson At The University of Michigan Dearborn As Prepared." Speech, University of Michigan-Dearborn, Dearborn, MI, January 13, 2016. https://www.dhs.gov/news/2016/01/15/remarks-secretary-homeland-security-jeh-johnson-university-michigan-dearborn

Context:

"Generations, like people, have personalities, and Millennials have begun to forge theirs: confident, self-expressive, liberal, upbeat, and open to change."[22] As optimistic as this is, it is important to note that this generation and the one below it is the demographic that is of interest to extremists and one that ISIL has exploited. They are aware that youth are, among other things, searching for belonging, navigating their identity, and looking for emotional connectivity and purpose. This period of discovery is compounded by adolescence and unique social-contextual factors. It is in this environment that extremist narratives find fertile soil. In the years since 9/11, this generation has experienced a unique set of factors that set them apart not the least of which is their exposure to a 24/7 media storm, instant images, likes, tweets, and sound bites from around the world and their peers. They are taking part in concurrent systems of influence and experiencing global events in new and personal ways. A significant number of violent extremists begin their radicalization process online where social media facilitates access to answers they are seeking and promotes a personal connection to those interested in ideological dialogue. Such connectivity to extremists online can turn to coordination of plans, and the development of both online and offline relationships as well as exposure to messages of opportunity, adventure, and purpose. Speaking of the three sisters radicalized by ISIL, Shiraz Maher describes the roots of radicalization like this: "It's identity, stupid."[23]

Regardless of the brand of extremist interested in winning them over, they are positioning their narratives to appeal to a sense of belonging, purpose, and identity. Whether the recruitment is by the Klu Klux Klan or that of ISIL, young people are targeted and persuaded around issues of belonging and identity. William McCants, a Senior Fellow at the Brookings Institution, commented, "Our brain may be wired to love our own group and dislike outsiders, but culture is the software that helps us determine who's in and who's out."[24] The cultural context in America is distinct from any other western nation, particularly around issues of identity. We should exploit this advantage in a real way. Beyond the rhetoric about American values, Millennials need to see, experience, and own their unique stories. Just presenting Americans as the most diverse nation in the world does not go far enough. We must help ignite the development of content where peers of different cultural upbringings have the opportunity to influence each other and create their own influential voices – both on and offline. Further, we have a unique opportunity to develop ethnically precise and very specific content marketing to segmented audiences delivered by grassroots partners However, the involvement of the government is an

---

[22] *Pew. Millennials: Confident. Connected. Open to Change"* Report. February 24, 2010.
http://www.pewsocialtrends.org/2010/02/24/millennials-confident-connected-open-to-change/.
[23] Maher, Shiraz. "The roots of radicalization? It's identity, stupid." *The Guardian*. June 17, 2015.
http://www.theguardian.com/commentisfree/2015/jun/17/roots-radicalisation-identity-bradford-jihadist-causes. *See Also:* Wood, Graeme. "What ISIS Really Wants." *The Atlantic*. March 2015.
http://www.theatlantic.com/magazine/archive/2015/03/what-isis-really-wants/384980/; Berger, J.M. "Enough about Islam: Why religion is not the most useful way to understand ISIS." Brookings. February 18, 2015.
http://www.brookings.edu/blogs/order-from-chaos/posts/2015/02/18-enough-about-islam-berger
[24] McCants, William. "How Terrorists Convince Themselves to Kill." *TIME*. December 10, 2015.
http://time.com/4144457/how-terrorists-kill/

immediate disqualifying and delegitimizing factor for any messaging campaign government, and will not have recognition by or resonance in the target audience. What does demonstrate success is the utilization of "influencers" with existing credibility and following, who can directly engage in both a broadcast as well as a direct dialogue with volume, tone, and content to which the target demographic will respond.[25]

Special attention should be focused on the use of "formers" – those who have been disengaged from the path to violent extremism – as credible messengers. Some international coalition partners have been quite successful in reducing recidivism and leveraging the voices and actions of disengaged extremists in countering narratives and working within at-risk communities. The U.S. Government should better understand the use of these voices and how to integrate them into programming.

Reaching Millennials through a variety of constructive, positive, and identity-building approaches will, in turn, encourage community and belonging within the greater American space. As we develop alternative narratives we must learn from mistakes in the past and recommit to finding new ways to offer the target audiences messages delivered through credible influencers (such as activists, peer leaders, actors, comedians, athletes and others). Further, cause-related marketing and initiatives that incorporate Millennials seamlessly and clearly into the greater American space, both online and in-person, offers great promise. This is either undertaken commensurately or followed closely by on-the-ground influences, with personal interaction between individuals, many of whom could be considered social influencers and/or who are positioned within particular networks of individuals who have demonstrated interest and willingness to join violent extremist organizations. These various factors may be determinative in mobilizing individuals to join or adopt to violent extremist groups, their messages, and their efforts. Our best hope to counter negative influence is positive influence, to offer alternatives to the propaganda of extremist groups, through which we may help young people find alternate pathways. In the development of alternative narratives and programs, government can have a role to play, but for a number of reasons, that role must be minimal.

Actions:

1. Leverage entrepreneurs from influencer communities, who may act as messengers, change-makers, or inspiration for their cohorts.
2. Facilitate the use of "formers" in CVE programming and messaging.
3. Build out networks of "former" violent extremists nationally from the wide array of groups including far right, anti-government, and other extremists groups seeking to radicalize and recruit.
4. Facilitate credible messenger and similar training of individuals in at-risk populations with social media and related companies, such as YouTube.
5. Work with the technology sector to amplify counter extremist content from diverse communities from across America and build grassroots campaigns to further this effort.

---

[25] Interview with Chris Graves and Shelina Janmohamed of Ogilvy Noor. May 20, 2016.

6. Create and implement a cohesive redesign of discussion around American history to puncture incorrect understanding of American history through partners such the Smithsonian, the Department of State's Bureau for Educational and Cultural Affairs, the Department of Education, and the Public Broadcasting Service, and other organizations and experts, to normalize cross-community conversation to eradicate ideas that any community is an "other."

7. Focus on gender diversity of youth through careful attention to the range of push and pull factors that attract individuals of differing gender.

8. Work with Department of State to scale effective programs that have already been funded by the U.S. Government to develop leadership skills and engage diverse youth change-agents and connect them to their American peers.

9. Work with think tanks that run international networks of change-makers and invest in long-term leadership development in key communities to build out American partnerships.

10. Re-examine existing legal and policy architecture to facilitate strategic communications within the United States based on content produced by other departments and agencies, and federally funded efforts.

11. Create a Virtual Department of Homeland Security Corps made up of university students modeled after the Department of State's Virtual Foreign Service.

CONCLUSION

Our nation's children will grow up in a world we could not have imagined a generation ago – a thriving world where human ingenuity and knowledge continues to expand by leaps and bounds. As that process of human evolution, including the expansion of freedom and liberties across the globe proceeds, our government must remain vigilant, adapt, and evolve to protect them.

We must do so by demonstrating faith in the American people, in their government, and we must be confident in the power of America's ideas. No new policy area, and no response to a historically unprecedented threat, comes without growing pains – and the Department will need to make difficult choices to adapt.

The recommendations in this report provide an overview of essential areas for countering efforts by extremists to radicalize, recruit, or mobilize followers to violence, including the conditions that allow violent extremist recruitment and radicalization to take hold. Foundational to each recommendation is embedded a belief that by acting as a convener, facilitator, and responsible financial partner, the government can help the American people defeat the threat of violent extremism. By looking clearly at what we need and what we must do to get there, we can build a sustainable architecture of engagement that incorporates all our tools and all the components that will protect our youth and future generations. This report is, by no means, an all-encompassing strategy – all components of the U.S. Government must coordinate their efforts to ensure that authorities are properly exercised. The Homeland is vital and central to all efforts. This report helps provide a basis for how the Department can more effectively organize and operationalize against the threat of violent extremism.

The Subcommittee thanks you for the opportunity to provide our thoughts and recommendations and stand ready to help the Department in any way.

Farah Pandith (Chair)
Adnan Kifayat (Chair)
General (Ret.) John Allen
Paul Goldenberg
Seamus Hughes
Joel T. Meyer
Jeffrey Miller
Michael Nutter
Matthew Olsen
Ali Soufan
Juan Zarate
William Webster (Ex-officio)

Appendix 1: Members of the Countering Violent Extremism (CVE) Subcommittee of the Homeland Security Advisory Council

Name	Title, Organization
Farah Pandith *(Chair)*	Adjunct Senior Fellow at the Council on Foreign Relations, Senior Fellow at the Kennedy School of Government at Harvard University, Former Special Representative to Muslim Communities, U.S. Department of State
Adnan Kifayat *(Chair)*	Senior Resident Fellow, German Marshall Fund of the United States, and Head of Global Security Ventures, Gen Next Foundation
John Allen	General, US Marine Corps (Ret.) and Co-Director, Center for 21st Century Security and Intelligence, the Brookings Institution
Paul Goldenberg	President and Chief Executive Officer, Cardinal Point Strategies
Seamus Hughes	Deputy Director, Program on Extremism at George Washington University
Joel T. Meyer	Senior Vice President, Public Sector at Dataminr
Jeffrey Miller	Senior Vice President and Chief Security Officer, National Football League
Michael Nutter	Former Mayor of Philadelphia, and David N. Dinkins Professor of Professional Practice of Urban & Public Policy, Columbia University/SIPA
Matthew Olsen	Co-Founder and President, Business Development, IronNet Cybersecurity
Ali Soufan	Chairman and Chief Executive Officer, The Soufan Group LLC
Juan Zarate	Chairman and Co-Founder, The Financial Integrity Network
William Webster *(Ex-officio)*	Retired Partner, Milbank, Tweed, Hadley & McCloy LLP

Members of the Department of Homeland Security Staff: Sarah Morgenthau, Erin Walls, and Lauren Wenger

Special Thanks to: Lila Ghosh, Ryan B. Greer, Michael Masters, Lauren Wenger, Erin Walls, and Alysha Tierney for their advice and assistance in compiling this report.

Appendix 2: Experts Consulted Include:

Individuals [26]

- Kevin Bearden, VP of Foreign Affairs, Federal Civilian Agencies for General Dynamics
- Charlotte Beers, Former Under Secretary for Public Diplomacy and Public Affairs, U.S. Department of State (2001-2003)
- Gene Beresin, MD, Executive Director, The Clay Center for Young Healthy Minds at Mass General Hospital
- Ambassador Matthew Bryza, Nonresident Senior Fellow, Atlantic Council
- Soraya Chemaly, Director, Women's Media Center Speech Project
- Kathleen Deloughery, Science and Technology Directorate, DHS
- Heidi Ellis, MD, Director, Center for Refugee Trauma and Resilience at Boston Children's Hospital
- Omar Fekeiki (Mahmood), Managing Editor, Raise Your Digital Voice at MBN
- Ambassador James Glassman, Former Under Secretary for Public Diplomacy and Public Affairs, U.S. Department of State (2008-2009)
- Christopher Graves, Global Chair, Ogilvy Public Relations
- Sasha Havlicek, Chief Executive Officer, Institute for Strategic Dialogue
- John Herman, MD, Associate Chief, Department of Psychiatry at Massachusetts General Hospital
- Shelina Janmohamed, Vice President, Ogilvy Noor
- Jonathan Keidan, Co-Founder and President, InsideHook
- Eric Kessler, Founder, Principal and Senior Managing Director, Arabella Advisors
- Imam Mohamed Magid, Executive Director, All Dulles Area Muslim Society
- Alisa Miller, PhD., Research Associate, Refugee Trauma and Resilience Center at Children's Hospital
- Hedieh Mirahmadi, President, World Organization for Resource Development and Education
- William Sabatini, General Manager, Radio Sawa
- Parisa Sabeti Zagat, Policy and Communications, Facebook
- Ron Schouten, MD, Director of the Law and Psychiatry Service, Massachusetts General Hospital
- George Selim, Director, the Office for Community Partnerships, DHS
- Tara Sonenshine, Former Under Secretary for Public Diplomacy and Public Affairs, U.S. Department of State (2012-2013)
- Peter Stern, Policy Manager for Risk, Facebook

---

[26] Individuals consulted did not necessarily speak on behalf of their organizations and their contributions should be viewed as theirs alone.

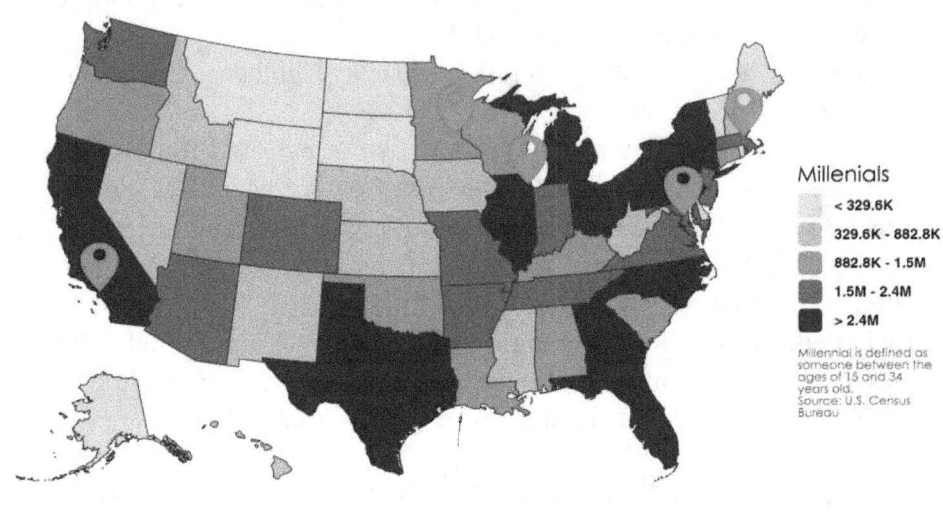

U.S. Government funded programs that seek to address violent extremism

Millenials

< 329.6K

329.6K - 882.8K

882.8K - 1.5M

1.5M - 2.4M

> 2.4M

Millennial is defined as someone between the ages of 15 and 34 years old.
Source: U.S. Census Bureau

Drop pins represent U.S. Government funded and/or financially supported programs that seek to explicitly address violent extremism. Please note that this list is representative but not necessarily exhaustive.

Milliennials' Social Media Use

Percentage of American 18-29 year olds who have accounts on social media platforms.

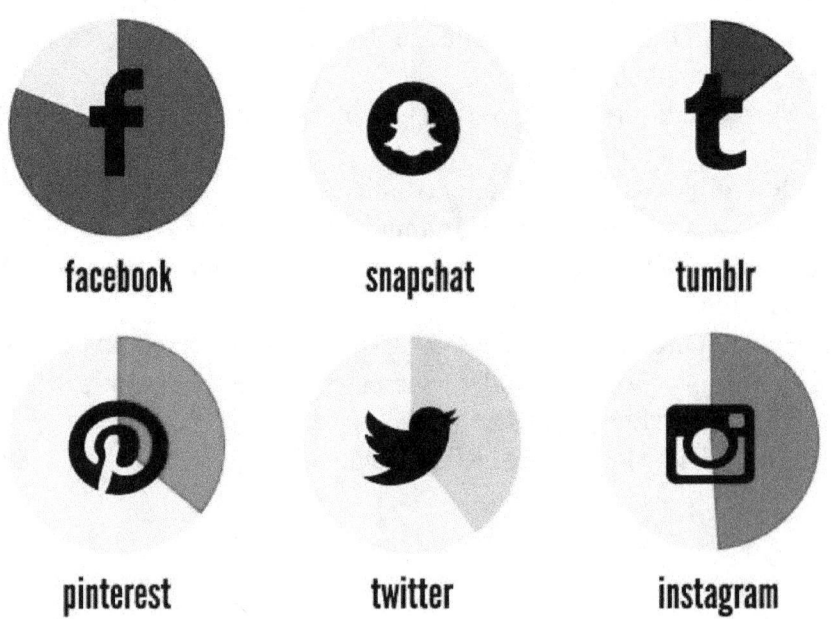

facebook   snapchat   tumblr

pinterest   twitter   instagram

Source: Harvard University Institute of Politics

Appendix 4: Relevant Reports and Recommendations

Beutel, Alejandro J. *Building Bridges to Strengthen America: Forging an Effective Counterterrorism Enterprise between Muslim Americans & Law Enforcement.* Executive Summary. Muslim Public Affairs Council. Recommendations:
   a) MPAC argues for a domestic counterterrorism enterprise centered on community-oriented policing.
   b) Law enforcement focuses on criminal behavior while communities address the ideological and social components which lead to violent extremism.
   c) Move away from a "securitized" relationship.

Briggs, Rachel and Sebastien Feve. *Policy Briefing: Countering the Appeal of Extremism Online.* Institute for Strategic Dialogue. Recommendations:
   a) Strengthening digital literacy and critical consumption among young people.
   b) Increasing counter-messaging, counter narrative, and alternative narrative activity. Government communications need to be centralized and coordinated. Governments need to be realistic about their ability to play an active messenger role and make significant investments in funding non-governmental organizations to offer credible alternatives.
   c) Building the capacity of credible messengers: governments should make investments in building skills and expertise of the most effective counter messengers. Governments should use their convening power to bring in private sector.

Davis, Thomas J. September 2014. *Now is the Time for CVE-2. Updating and Implementing a Revised U.S. National Strategy to Counter Violent Extremism.* Naval Postgraduate School. Recommendations:
   a) Identifying the federal agency in charge of administering the U.S. CVE strategy.
   b) Developing a more robust and actionable national CVE framework.
   c) Refocusing the federal government on support and not local engagement of CVE.
   d) Requiring all CVE related terms be defined in every document.
   e) Requiring regular evaluations and updates of the U.S. CVE strategy.

Department of State, and USAID. Department of State & USAID Joint Strategy on Countering Violent Extremism. Report. May 2016. Recommendations:
   a) Enhance CVE diplomacy.
   b) Focus on CVE strategic communications.
   c) Expand rule of law and develop programs to advance CVE.
   d) Promote research and learning.
   e) Elevate CVE within broader U.S. foreign policy.

Muslim Public Affairs Council. *Policy Report: Data on Post-9/11 Terrorism in the United States.* Recommendations:
   a) Expand community-oriented policing initiatives.
   b) Increase support for research on combating biased policing.
   c) Expand investments in better human capital acquisitions.

d) Highlight citizen contributions to national security.
e) Reform the fusion center process to increase coordination among law enforcement. Adopt MPAC's "four essential principles" to successful engagement with Muslim American communities.

U.S. Department of Homeland Security. *American Foreign Fighters: Implications for Homeland Security Final Report.* August 31, 2015. Pages 43-44. Publication RP14-01.03.11-01. Recommendations:
a) Countering Violent Extremism (CVE) efforts can be strengthened by incorporating travel behaviors of foreign fighters.
b) Relying on a range of international, federal, state, local, community partners, and families is critical for the U.S. to continue focusing on efforts to identify potential foreign fighters as early as possible.

Vidino, Lorenzo and Seamus Hughes. *Countering Violent Extremism in America.* The George Washington University Center for Cyber & Homeland Security: Program on Extremism. Recommendations:
a) If the U.S. government truly wants to engage in robust CVE, it will need to provide sufficient funding.
b) The administration should appoint one department as the lead for CVE efforts to ensure more focused programs and a single point of contact for public advocacy and congressional oversight.
c) Engagement and other trust-building initiatives are useful and should be continued.
d) Build trust in American Muslim communities.
e) Develop accountability for CVE at the federal level.

Appendix 5: Glossary

Countering Violent Extremism (CVE): Actions to counter efforts by extremists to radicalize, recruit, or mobilize followers to violence and to address the conditions that allow violent extremist recruitment and radicalization.

Credible Messengers: Individuals or organizations that have the ability and authority to influence audiences. Whether they are religious leaders, teachers, parents, pop culture idols, those who are the best placed to create change are those whom CVE efforts must prioritize.

ISIL: The Islamic State of Iraq and the Levant.

Disengagement: The process whereby an individual experiences a change in role or function that is usually associated with a reduction of violent participation. It may not necessarily involve leaving the movement, but is most frequently associated with significant temporary or permanent role change. Additionally, while disengagement may stem from role change, that role change may be influenced by psychological factors such as disillusionment, burnout or the failure to reach the expectations that influenced initial involvement. This can lead to a member seeking out a different role within the movement.[27]

Formers: Individuals who have been involved in violent extremism but have become rehabilitated and offered to serve as credible messengers in CVE programming.

Network: Offices; organizations; communities associated based on location, ethnicity, or some other demographic association. Communities of disenfranchised individuals and those who influence them will represent those for whom CVE programming will be scoped and by whom it should be carried out; creating connectivity across these individuals will be paramount for success.

Platform: A technological tool or organizational mechanism to facilitate coordination or communication. Platforms will enable cross-sector and interagency cohesion for efforts.

Radicalization: The social and psychological process of incrementally experienced commitment to extremist political or religious ideology. Radicalization may not necessary lead to violence but it is one of the several risk factors required for this.[28]

Violent Extremist: An individual who supports or commits ideologically-motivated violence to further political goals.

---

[27] Horgan, John, and Kurt Braddock. "Rehabilitating the Terrorists?: Challenges in Assessing the Effectiveness of De-radicalization Programs." *Terrorism and Political Violence* 22 (2010): 267-91.
[28] *Ibid.*

Appendix 6: Bibliography

Anne Aly, Elisabeth Taylor & Saul Karnovsky (2014) "Moral Disengagement and Building Resilience to Violent Extremism: An Education Intervention", Studies in Conflict & Terrorism, 37:4, 369-385, DOI: 10.1080/1057610X.2014.879379

Belasco, Amy. "The Cost of Iraq, Afghanistan, and Other Global War on Terror Operations Since 9/11." Congressional Research Service. December 8, 2014

Berger, J.M. and Morgan, Jonathan. "The ISIS Twitter Consensus: Defining and describing the population of ISIS on Twitter." Brookings Institution. The Brookings Project on U.S. Relations with the Islamic World. March 2015.

Berger, J.M. "Enough about Islam: Why Religion Is Not the Most Useful Way to Understand ISIS." *Brookings* (blog), February 18, 2015. Accessed May 25, 2016. http://www.brookings.edu/blogs/order-from-chaos/posts/2015/02/18-enough-about-islam-berger.

Beutel, Alejandro J. "Building Bridges to Strengthen America: Forging an Effective Counterterrorism Enterprise between Muslim Americans & Law Enforcement. Executive Summary." Muslim Public Affairs Council.

Bhui et al.: "A public health approach to understanding and preventing violent radicalization." BMC Medicine 2012 10:16.

Boston Children's Hospital, UMass Lowell, Minerva Initiative, and National Institute of Justice. "Methods for Successful Research Related to Violent Extremism N the Somali-American Community." Report. February 12, 2015. Accessed May 26, 2016. http://bit.ly/1U9aK7N

Boston Children's Hospital, UMass Lowell, Minerva Initiative, and National Institute of Justice. "Pathways to and away from Violent Extremism among Somalis in North America." Report. February 13, 2015. Accessed May 26, 2016. http://bit.ly/1VjKFZ1

Briggs, Rachel and Sebastien Feve. "Policy Briefing: Countering the Appeal of Extremism Online." Institute for Strategic Dialogue.

Carpenter, J. Scott, Matthew Levitt, Steven Simon, and Juan Zarate. *Fighting the Ideological Battle: The Missing Link in U.S. Strategy to Counter Violent Extremism.* Report. The Washington Institute. July 2010. Accessed May 25, 2016.

Coolsaet, Rik. "Facing the Fourth Foreign Fighters Wave: What Drives Europeans to Syria, and to the Islamic State? Insights from the Belgian Case?" Egmont: Royal Institute for International Relations. Report. March 2016. Accessed May 25, 2016. http://www.egmontinstitute.be/wp-content/uploads/2016/02/egmont.papers.81_online-versie.pdf.

Davis, Thomas J. "Now is the Time for CVE-2. Updating and Implementing a Revised U.S. National Strategy to Counter Violent Extremism." Naval Postgraduate School. September 2014.

Department of Homeland Security, Homeland Security Advisory Committee. "Countering Violent Extremism Working Group." Spring 2010.. http://bit.ly/27VFraR

Department of Homeland Security, Homeland Security Advisory Committee. "Foreign Fighter Task Force Interim Report." Spring 2015.

Department of Homeland Security. "Montgomery County Model." https://www.dhs.gov/sites/default/files/publications/Montgomery%20County%20MD%20Community%20Partnership%20Model-WORDE%20Report.pdf

Department of Homeland Security. "Statement by Secretary Jeh C. Johnson on DHS's New Office for Community Partnerships." September 28, 2015.

Department of Homeland Security. "Terminology to Define the Terrorists: Recommendations from American Muslims." Office of Civil Rights and Civil Liberties. January 2008.

Department of State, and USAID. "Department of State & USAID Joint Strategy on Countering Violent Extremism." Report. May 2016. Accessed May 26, 2016. http://www.state.gov/documents/organization/257913.pdf.

Ellis, B. H., Abdi, S. M., Lazarevic, V., White, M. T., Lincoln, A. K., Stern, J. E., & Horgan, J. G.(2015, November 30)." Relation of Psychosocial Factors to Diverse Behaviors and Attitudes Among Somali Refugees." American Journal of Orthopsychiatry. Advance. online publication. http://dx.doi.org/10.1037/ort0000121

Feddes, Allard R., Liesbeth Mann, and Bertjan Doosje. "Increasing Self-esteem and Empathy to Prevent Violent." Journal of Applied Social Psychology 45 (2015): 400-11.

Harvard University's Institute of Politics. "Harvard IOP Spring 2016 Poll." Report. April 25, 2016. Accessed May 25, 2016. http://iop.harvard.edu/youth-poll/harvard-iop-spring-2016-poll.

Hazen, Eric, Steven Schlozman, and Eugene Beresin. "Adolescent Psychological Development: A Review." Pediatrics in Review 29, no. 5 (May 2008): 161-68. http://pedsinreview.aappublications.org/cgi/content/full/29/5/161

Hedayah, and International Centre for Counter-Terrorism - The Hague. "Developing Effective Counter-Narrative." September 2014. Meeting Note

Horgan, John, and Kurt Braddock. "Rehabilitating the Terrorists?: Challenges in Assessing the Effectiveness of De-radicalization Programs." *Terrorism and Political Violence* 22 (2010): 267-91. Accessed May 25, 2016. https://www.start.umd.edu/sites/default/files/files/publications/Derad.pdf.

Interview with Chris Graves and Shelina Janmohamed of Ogilvy Noor. May 20, 2016.

Interview with Ron Schouten, MD, Director of the Law and Psychiatry Service, Massachusetts General Hospital

Johnson, Secretary Jeh. "Remarks By Secretary of Homeland Security Jeh Johnson At The University of Michigan Dearborn As Prepared." Speech, University of Michigan-Dearborn, Dearborn, MI, January 13, 2016. https://www.dhs.gov/news/2016/01/15/remarks-secretary-homeland-security-jeh-johnson-university-michigan-dearborn

Maher, Shiraz. "The roots of radicalization? It's identity, stupid." *The Guardian*. June 17, 2015. http://www.theguardian.com/commentisfree/2015/jun/17/roots-radicalisation-identity-bradford-jihadist-causes.

McCants, William. "How Terrorists Convince Themselves to Kill." *Time*, December 10, 2015. Accessed May 25, 2016. http://time.com/4144457/how-terrorists-kill/.

Muslim Public Affairs Council. Policy Report: "Data on Post-9/11 Terrorism in the United States." 23 April 2013. http://www.mpac.org/publications/policy-papers/post-911-terrorism-database.php

Nutter, Michael. "Proposal for the Creation of a National Commission on Domestic, Terrorism, Violence and Crime in America." January 2013.

Nye, Joseph S. "Soft Power." *Foreign Policy*, no. 80 (1990): 153-71.

Perliger, Arie and Pedahzur, Ami, "Social Network Analysis in the Study of Terrorism and Political Violence" (2010). Working Papers. Paper 48. http://opensiuc.lib.siu.edu/pn_wp/48

Program on Extremism at the George Washington University. Report. "April 2016." Accessed May 25, 2016. https://cchs.gwu.edu/sites/cchs.gwu.edu/files/downloads/April Report Update.pdf.

"Racist Group Begins Youth Recruitment Effort." Anti-Defamation League, January 12, 2015. http://blog.adl.org/extremism/white-supremacist-group-begins-youth-recruitment-effort.

Ressler, Steve. "Social Network Analysis as an Approach to Combat Terrorism: Past, Present, and Future Research." Homeland Security Affairs 2, Article 8 (July 2006). https://www.hsaj.org/articles/171

Rewriting the Narrative: An Integrated Strategy for Counter radicalization. Report. The Washington Institute. March 2009. Accessed May 25, 2016. http://www.washingtoninstitute.org/uploads/Documents/pubs/PTF2-Counterradicalization.pdf.

Sparrow, Malcolm K. "The Application of Network Analysis to Criminal Intelligence: An Assessment of the Prospects." Social Networks 13, no. 3 (September 1991): 251-74.

START. *Overview: Profiles of Individual Radicalization in the United States - Foreign Fighters (PIRUS-FF).* Issue brief. April 2016. Accessed May 25, 2016. https://www.start.umd.edu/pubs/START_PIRUS-FF_InfographicSeries_April2016.pdf.

The White House. "Empowering Local Partners to Prevent Violent Extremism in the United States." August 2011.

The White House. Office of the Press Secretary. "Fact Sheet: The 2015 National Security Strategy." News release, February 6, 2015. The White House. https://www.whitehouse.gov/the-press-office/2015/02/06/fact-sheet-2015-national-security-strategy.

Tucker, David. "Terrorism, Networks, and Strategy: Why the Conventional Wisdom is Wrong." Homeland Security Affairs 4, Article 5 (June 2008). https://www.hsaj.org/articles/122

United States Census Bureau. "ACS DEMOGRAPHIC AND HOUSING ESTIMATES." 2014. Raw data. http://1.usa.gov/1WWSXrt

United States Census Bureau. "Millennials Outnumber Baby Boomers and Are Far More Diverse, Census Bureau Reports." News release, June 25, 2015. Accessed May 25, 2016. https://www.census.gov/newsroom/press-releases/2015/cb15-113.html.

United States. Department of Homeland Security. "American Foreign Fighters: Implications for Homeland Security Final Report." August 31, 2015. Pages 43-44. Publication RP14-01.03.11-01.

United States. Department of Homeland Security. Office for Civil Rights and Civil Liberties. "TERMINOLOGY TO DEFINE THE TERRORISTS: RECOMMENDATIONS FROM AMERICAN MUSLIMS." January 2008. Accessed May 25, 2016. https://www.dhs.gov/xlibrary/assets/dhs_crcl_terminology_08-1-08_accessible.pdf.

Vidino, Lorenzo and Seamus Hughes. "Countering Violent Extremism in America." The George Washington University Center for Cyber & Homeland Security: Program on Extremism. December 2015.

Wood, Graeme. "What ISIS Really Wants." *The Atlantic*. Accessed May 25, 2016. http://www.theatlantic.com/magazine/archive/2015/03/what-isis-really-wants/384980/.

Wood, Graeme. "'What ISIS Really Wants': The Response." *The Atlantic*, February 24, 2015. Accessed May 25, 2016. http://www.theatlantic.com/international/archive/2015/02/what-isis-really-wants-reader-response-atlantic/385710/.

www.ingramcontent.com/pod-product-compliance
Lightning Source LLC
Chambersburg PA
CBHW081538280526
45788CB00010B/3284